A VISIT TO
Costa Rica

REVISED AND UPDATED

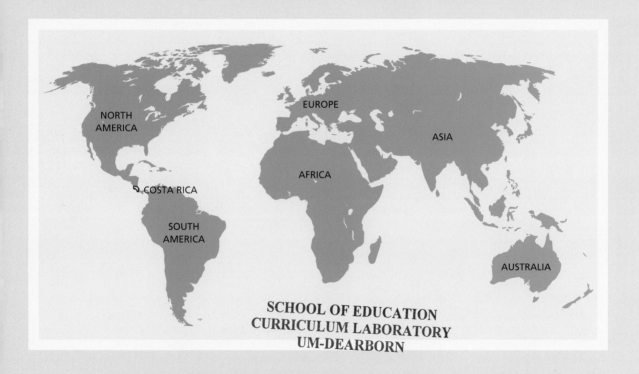

NORTH AMERICA

EUROPE

ASIA

AFRICA

COSTA RICA

SOUTH AMERICA

AUSTRALIA

SCHOOL OF EDUCATION
CURRICULUM LABORATORY
UM-DEARBORN

Mary Virginia Fox

Heinemann Library
Chicago, Illinois

© 2001, 2009 Heinemann Library
a division of Pearson Inc.
Chicago, Illinois

Customer Service 888-454-2279
Visit our website at www.heinemannraintree.com

Designed by Joanna Hinton-Malivoire
Printed in China by South China Printing Company Limited

13 12 11 10 09
10 9 8 7 6 5 4 3 2 1

New edition ISBN-10:1-4329-1281-X (hardcover), 1-4329-1300-X (paperback)
New edition ISBN-13: 978-1-4329-1281-9 (hardcover), 978-1-4329-1300-7 (paperback)

The Library of Congress has cataloged the first edition as follows:
Fox, Mary Virginia.
         Costa Rica / Mary Virginia Fox.
                  p. cm. – (A visit to)
         Includes bibliographical references and index.
         Summary: An introduction to the land, culture, and people of Costa Rica.
         ISBN 1-57572-379-4 (library binding)
         1. Costa Rica—Description and travel—Juvenile literature. [1. Costa Rica.] I. Title. II. Series.

F1544.F69 2000
972.86—dc21   00-029548

Acknowledgments
The publishers would like to thank the following for permission to reproduce photographs: © Aurora
p. **16** (PictureQuest/Peter Essick); © Corbis pp. **5** (Martin Rogers), **6** (Dave G. Houser), **8** (Martin
Rogers), **9** (Michael and Patricia Fogden), **10** (Martin Rogers), **11** (Gary Braasch), **13** (The Purcell
Team), **14** (Martin Rogers), **17** (Martin Rogers), **20** (The Purcell Team), **21** (Kit Kittle), **23** (Martin
Rogers), **24** (Martin Rogers), **25** (Joel W. Rogers), **27** (Martin Rogers); © Getty Images (AFP/Yuri
Cortez) pp. **15**, **26**, **29**; © National Geographic Image Collection p. **28**; © Photolibrary Group (Robert
Harding/RH Productions) pp. **12**, **18**, **19**, **22**; © Tony Stone Images p. **7** (Tom Benoit).

Cover photograph reproduced with permission of © Getty Images (The Image Bank/Jerry Driendl).

Every effort has been made to contact copyright holders of any material reproduced in this book. Any
omissions will be rectified in subsequent printings if notice is given to the publisher.

Contents

Any words appearing in bold, **like this**, are explained in the Glossary.

Costa Rica

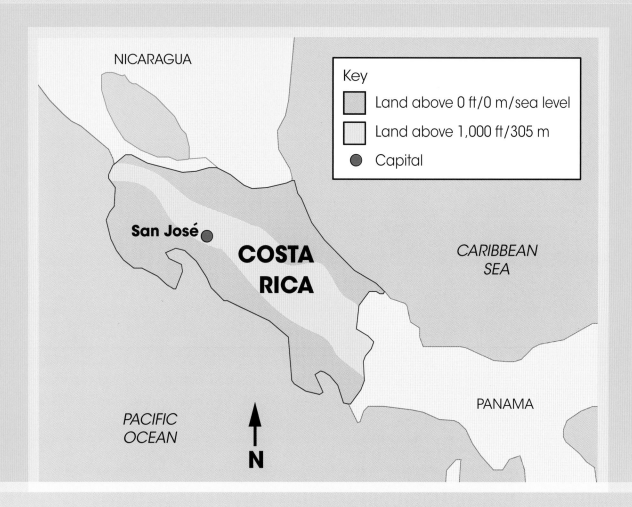

Key
- Land above 0 ft/0 m/sea level
- Land above 1,000 ft/305 m
- ● Capital

NICARAGUA

San José ●

COSTA RICA

CARIBBEAN SEA

PANAMA

PACIFIC OCEAN

N

Costa Rica is in **Central America**. It has one **coast** on the Caribbean Sea and one coast on the Pacific Ocean.

The name Costa Rica means "rich coast." It is a beautiful country. People like to go there on vacation.

Costa Rica has low **plains** and **tropical rain forests** along both **coasts**. Here the weather is very warm.

In the middle of the country there are high mountains. Costa Rica also has **volcanoes**. They sometimes cover nearby homes and fields with ash.

Arenal is one of the most active volcanoes in Costa Rica.

Landmarks

The **capital** of Costa Rica is San José. The people of Costa Rica are proud of their beautiful churches. Some were built more than 300 years ago.

Monteverde means "green mountain."

People from all over the world come to see the Monteverde cloud **rain forest.** Trees and plants grow on hills that are often covered by clouds. Many birds and animals live here.

Homes

In the middle of the country, houses are made of **concrete** blocks. They can stand up to storms and hurricanes. The houses are often painted bright colors.

In the cities, many people live in apartments or houses. Closer to the **coasts**, houses are often built on **stilts** to keep them from flooding.

Houses by the coast are often made of wood.

Food

Many fruits grow in Costa Rica. People like to eat bananas and mangos. They also eat melons, oranges, and pineapples.

Rice may be part of breakfast, lunch, or dinner.

Red and white beans mixed with rice, onions, and **spices** are a favorite food. Soups and stews made with meat, vegetables, and rice are also popular.

Clothes

People in Costa Rica wear modern clothes such as jeans or shorts and T-shirts. Children in some schools wear uniforms.

For special celebrations, some women and girls wear full skirts and ruffled blouses. Men often wear straw hats shaped like cowboy hats.

Bananas and coffee are two **crops** that are grown in Costa Rica. Workers pick coffee berries by hand. There are coffee beans inside the berries.

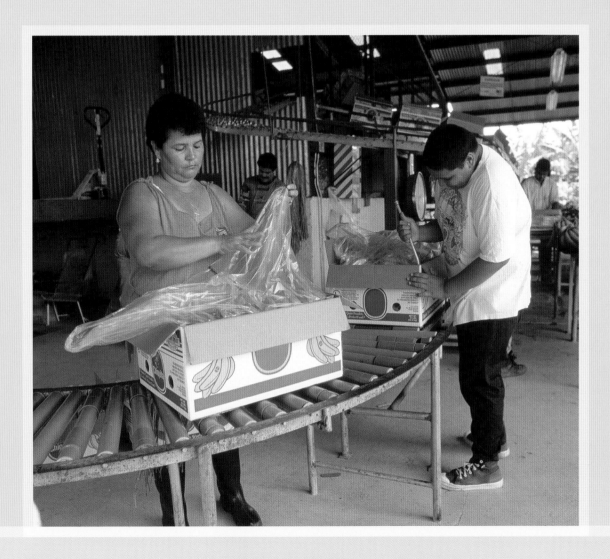

There are many factories in Costa Rica. Some are for packing fruits and vegetables. Other factories make instant coffee. These products are also sold in other countries.

Transportation

In the cities, many people drive cars. On country roads, people often ride horses. **Oxen** pull carts that carry heavy farm loads.

Big trucks carry crops and products along the highway.

A long highway goes through Costa Rica. It connects Costa Rica with other countries in **Central America**.

Language

In Costa Rica, most people speak Spanish. This is because Costa Rica was **settled** by people from Spain. Many people also speak English. Often, words from both languages are used together.

When Costa Ricans go inside someone's house, they might say, *con permiso*. This is a way of asking permission to go in. Some people call each other *mi amor*. It means "my love." It is a friendly form of greeting.

School

Children start school when they are five years old. They study Spanish, English, and many other subjects. Some children eat their lunches in the classroom.

The school year begins in March and ends in November. There is a two-week vacation in July.

Soccer is very popular. In Costa Rica, it is called football. Horseback riding is a sport and a way to get around. Races are sometimes held between villages.

Many places in Costa Rica are near the water. People go to Costa Rica for **surfing**. They also raft and **kayak** in the rivers.

Celebrations

There are many **fiestas** and fairs during the year. On October 12, people celebrate the day Christopher Columbus arrived in America. This holiday is called *El día de la raza.*

Many people in Costa Rica are Roman Catholic, so religious holidays are very important. Some holidays celebrate the special days of people called **saints**.

The Arts

The **native people** of Costa Rica left many kinds of art. There are huge balls that were carved from stone. Other people carved beautiful statues with a stone called jade.

This artist is getting ready to take part in the Summer Festival in San José.

Art doesn't always have to be shown in museums. Some people in Costa Rica like to make everyday things into works of art.

29

Fact File

Name The Republic of Costa Rica is the country's full name.

Capital The **capital** of the country is San José.

Language Most people in Costa Rica speak Spanish.

Population There are about four million people living in Costa Rica.

Money The money in Costa Rica is called the colón.

Religions Most people belong to the Roman Catholic Church.

Products **Crops** such as **sugarcane**, coffee, bananas, and pineapples grow in Costa Rica. Clothes and shoes are made, along with some small electric appliances.

Words you can learn

adiós (ah-dee-OS)	goodbye
maje (MAH-hay)	buddy, pal
pura vida (POO-ra VEE-dah)	okay
sí (see)	yes
gracias (GRAH-see-yahs)	thank you
buenos días (BWAY-nohs DEE-yahs)	good morning
buenas noches (BWAY-nahs NOH-chez)	good night
con permiso (cohn pair-MEE-so)	may I?
mi amor (mee ah-MOHR)	my love

Glossary

capital important city where the government is based

Central America land between Panama and Mexico

coast land at the edge of an ocean

concrete manufactured stone used to make buildings

crop plant that is grown for food

fiesta holiday fair or party

kayak small boat with one long oar that has a paddle at each end

ox large animal that is very strong. More than one are called oxen.

plain flat land often covered in grass or small bushes

port place where boats can stay

rain forest deep woods with tall trees where rain often falls

saint person who lived in a very good and holy way

settled moved from one country to live in another country

spice dried, ground-up plant used to flavor foods

stilts supports that are like legs

sugarcane kind of tall grass that can be made into sugar

surfing riding the waves on a special board

tropical hot and wet

unique different in a special way

volcano mountain that has been formed by hot rocks pushing up through the ground and that can blow out hot smoke or fire and ashes

Index